Lucy
THE ADVENTURER

Published in 2022
First published in the UK by THP Kidz Zone
An imprint of Tamarind Hill Press Limited
Newton Aycliffe, County Durham, DL5 6XP
Copyright © Dusty Sticks
All rights reserved

ISBN: 978-1-915161-15-4

Email business@tamarindhillpress.com for bulk orders

Lucy
THE
ADVENTURER

by
DUSTY STICKS

Lucy Gosling is your typical kid adventurer.

She is brave, smart, and always looking for something new to discover.

The world is an exciting place, and Lucy wants to see every part of it.

Lucy's parents fly all over.

Their job is to write about all the wonderful places they visit.

Thanks to them, Lucy has been able to go to some of the most amazing places in the world.

One time, Lucy and her family went to Vietnam.

There, Lucy got to explore the Son Doong cave.

This is the largest cave in the world, big enough to fit an entire city inside it.

The early parts of the cave are covered in beautiful lakes and trees.

Then when you go deeper, there's no light, so you have to bring your own lantern to stay safe.

There was one spring when Lucy and her family went to Canada.

They were there to see the Monarch butterfly migration.

Thousands of butterflies get together and fly around to enjoy the warm weather and lay their eggs.

There are so many of them, that you can barely see the sky!

They go there because it's where they can find their favorite plant, milkweed.

When Lucy stood very still, a butterfly landed right on her finger.

For summer, everyone went to Laguna Beach in California.

There are so many tidepools there! Those are pools that form by on the beach.

They're filled with all sorts of amazing plants and animals from the ocean.

If it wasn't for the tide pools, you might not get to see them.

Lucy found some sea anemones in one of the pools.

They're cool to look at, but they'll sting if you touch them.

Lucy wouldn't be able to travel the world on her own.

Her parents are why Lucy can fly all over the world.

And thanks to Lucy's brother, Ryder, she always had a way to get where she wants to go.

Ryder can ride any animal in the world.

He can ride horses to get them across open plains.

He can have camels help them across the hot, hot deserts.

He can even ride mules that get them over any mountain.

No matter where it is, Ryder always knows how to get to the best places to visit.

But some of Lucy's best adventures happen right at home.

Lucy will go outside and try to look for one new thing that she's never seen before.

She'll almost always find something new.

Lucy will find a new bug, a bird, or a plant.

And as soon as she sees it, she'll write about it in her journal.

She'll draw what it looks like, and write down where she found it so she can find it later.

If Lucy's lucky, she'll even find a new place in the woods.

Like a small pond full of new things for her to explore!

Lucy is a lucky kid who gets to travel over the world.

But every good adventurer knows that you can have an adventure anywhere, even in your own backyard.

You can have an adventure yourself!

Go outside and try to find one new thing.

Or go online and try to learn something cool about a plant, an animal, or a place.

The world is full of adventure, you just need to know how to find them.

Then anyone can be an adventurer, just like Lucy.

www.ingramcontent.com/pod-product-compliance
Lightning Source LLC
Chambersburg PA
CBHW051318110526
44590CB00031B/4397